The Centurion at the Cross

The story of Good Friday and Easter Sunday

Matthew 27:45–54

Luke 22:63–23:49
for children

Written by Eric Bohnet
Illustrated by Terri Murphy

Arch® Books
Copyright © 2007 Concordia Publishing House
3558 S. Jefferson Avenue, St. Louis, MO 63118-3968
1-800-325-3040 • www.cph.org
Manufactured in Colombia

They call me a centurion,
An officer from Rome.
I'm stationed in Jerusalem,
A long way from my home.

That's where I learned of God's great love.
It was for me outpoured
That day when I did crucify
His Son, Jesus, my Lord.

I led my men to Pilate's house
That fateful Friday morn.
I noticed that the crowds were big,
And Pilate looked forlorn.

I asked of Pilate, "What's the charge?
Why's this one paying dues?"
He told me I could read the sign.
It said "King of the Jews."

"A rebel, eh?" I answered back.
He sadly shook his head.
"That's what their priests and leaders say;
They sure do want Him dead."

I saw that Jesus had been scourged;
His back was red and torn
And on His head, to mock the "king,"
A crown made out of thorns.

And yet He did look like a king
Through all the blood and pain.
His eyes looked back at me with love
That I could not explain.

I wished that I could spare this man,
Not lead Him off to die.
But still I led Him out of town
Up to a hill so high.

My men stretched out His hands and feet
And nailed Him to the tree.
He screamed, and then I heard the priests
And leaders shout with glee.

I wished that I could take those priests
And nail them up there too.
But Jesus cried, "Father, forgive!
They know not what they do."

"Forgive?" For all they'd done to Him?
Nailing Him up to die?
But then I knew He meant me too,
And could not help but cry.

At noon that day the sky turned black—
'Twas dark as deepest night.
I wondered where the sun had gone
And why there was no light.

I watched Him speak with kindness to
His mother and a thief,
Although He hung in agony
And pain beyond belief.

He suffered all that afternoon
In darkness all alone,
But finally He'd had enough.
"I thirst," I heard Him groan.

A look of triumph filled His face.
"It's finished," Jesus cried.
Just then an earthquake shook the ground,
And I saw that He'd died.

No longer could I keep my peace
About what He had done:
"Surely this man was innocent;
This man was God's own Son!"

And that's how Jesus conquered death,
For He soon rose again.
He died to save us from our sins
And take us home to heaven.

Dear Parent:

We know that a centurion was an officer in the Roman army, possibly commanding as many as 100 soldiers. Although the Bible doesn't say much about the centurion, in our story, he didn't want to kill Jesus, but he obeyed Pontius Pilate, the Roman governor, and ordered his men to crucify Him anyway. As a soldier, he would have been trained to follow orders. And as a military officer, he may have been reluctant to lose his prestigious job.

Regardless why he ordered the crucifixion, the centurion did acknowledge that he was also guilty of Jesus' death. He was just as guilty as the Jewish priests who condemned Jesus and the soldiers who actually nailed Him to the cross. When Jesus said, "Father, forgive," the centurion knew that Jesus forgave all the people responsible for His death.

Ask your child if she's ever been asked to do something she knew was wrong. Maybe her friends encouraged her to break a rule at school or tried to get her to disobey at home. Explain that while it's easy to say no when people ask you to do something that is obviously wrong, there are times that breaking one little rule or a minor disobedience will seem to be okay. Tell your child that when she does something wrong, she will still have to endure the consequences of her action. But explain that when we acknowledge our sin and repent from it, Jesus forgives our sins just as He forgave the priests, the Roman soldiers, and the centurion. Jesus died and rose from the dead to take the eternal punishment for the world's sins. Now we can be forgiven and have eternal life with Him in heaven.

The Editor